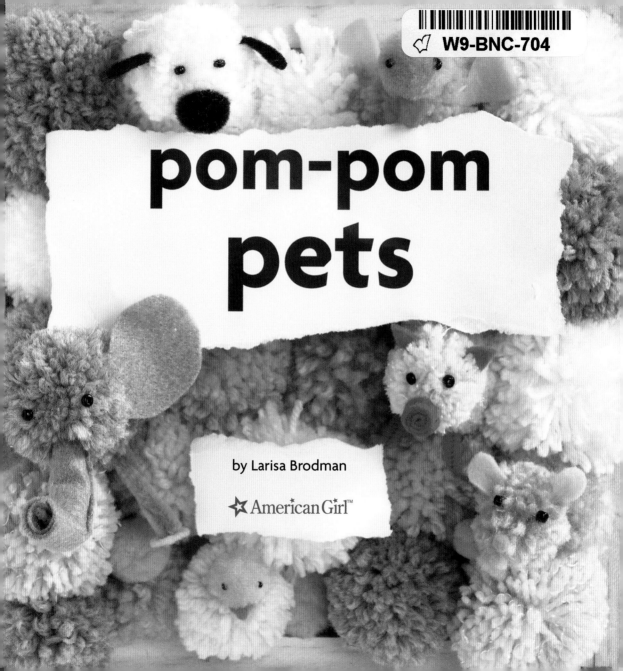

pom-pom pets

by Larisa Brodman

★ American Girl™

Published by Pleasant Company Publications

Copyright © 2006 by American Girl, LLC

Questions or comments? Call 1-800-845-0005,
visit our Web site at **americangirl.com,**
or write to Customer Service, American Girl, 8400 Fairway Place, Middleton, WI 53562-0497.

Printed in China

06 07 08 09 10 11 LEO 10 9 8 7 6 5 4 3 2

American Girl™ and its associated logos are trademarks of American Girl, LLC.

Editorial Development: Trula Magruder

Art Direction and Design: Camela Decaire

Production: Jeannette Bailey, Judith Lary, Gail Longworth, Mindy Rappe, Kendra Schluter

Tabletop photography: Radlund Photography

Stylist: Camela Decaire

Special thanks to Nicole R.

Special thanks to our testers: Alexandra M.; Bridget A.; Gabriela S.; Katie B.;
Kelsey H.; Kelsey H.; Maura M.; Payton B.; Samantha A.; Taylor B.

Photographic backgrounds: pages 11, 13, 17, 25, 35, 37, 45, Fotosearch; page 15, © Stone/Getty Images; pages 19, 21, 33, 46 Getty Images; page 23, © Dale C Spartas/Corbis; page 27, 47, © Taxi/Getty Images; page 29, © Botanica/Getty Images; page 31, © Digital Vision/Fotosearch; page 39, © National Georgraphic/ Getty Images; page 43, © Stone/Getty Images

dear reader,

Capture the fuzz, feathers, and fur of your favorite animals with pom-poms! Use the pom-pom makers, pretty yarns, chenille stems, and other kit supplies to create a variety of fluffy, puffy, and cuddly creatures. Then share your animals with family and friends. Here are a few ideas:

- Pack a polar bear into a Christmas stocking.
- Slip a bunny into an Easter basket.
- Pass out sheep at a sleepover.
- Put a poodle on a pillow for a sick pal.
- Give a cousin a kitten for Hanukkah.
- Offer an owl to a favorite teacher.
- Attach a cow to a card for a friend who's moo-ving.

Just let your imagination run wild!

your friends at American Girl

in your kit

pom-pom makers

Each pom-pom maker creates a different-sized pom-pom.

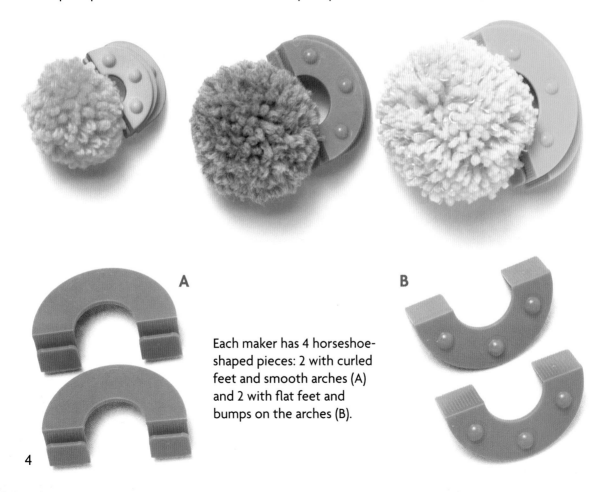

A

B

Each maker has 4 horseshoe-shaped pieces: 2 with curled feet and smooth arches (A) and 2 with flat feet and bumps on the arches (B).

chenille stems

For legs and tails, your kit has 3 kinds of stems: fuzzy, plain, and bumpy. Try other types, such as curly or striped.

Caution: Cutting chenille stems can cause sharp ends and scratch or cut skin, so be careful handling them.

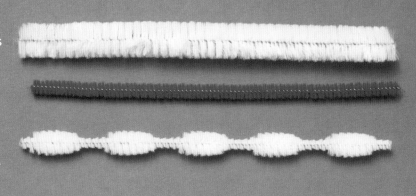

premade pom-poms

You'll find these sizes in your kit. You can find many other sizes, including x-large, at craft stores.

mini   **x-small**   **small**   **medium**   **large**

yarn

This kit has some yarns. You can also use leftover from knitting projects or buy yarn at craft stores.

seed beads

Some animals will need small beads for eyes and some will need larger beads.

felt squares

Use felt for ears, tails, and more!

make a pom-pom!

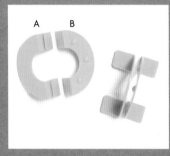

1. Place piece A with piece B so that the pieces stand up as shown. Repeat with second pair.

2. Pick up 1 pair. Press 2 halves together while holding a long tail of yarn against maker with thumb.

3. Starting anywhere on arch, wrap yarn from side to side. Wrap until entire arch is covered, as shown.

4. Cut yarn. (Don't worry about loose ends.) Repeat steps 2 and 3 with second pair.

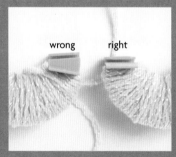

5. Before continuing, make sure to line up feet so that they're level. Tip: You may need to twist maker.

6. Slide curled feet of one half into flat feet of other half to make a circle. Tip: You may need to wiggle pieces.

7. Your pom-pom should look like this!

8. Starting near feet, slip scissor points into slot between piece A and piece B. Cut all yarn layers along slot of arch.

9. Cut a long piece of yarn. Slide it into slot, as shown.

10. Tie a double knot, pulling yarn until it's tight against pom-pom.

11. Separate feet, then gently tug apart each half of pom-pom maker.

12. Trim longer yarn pieces to make a ball. Fluff.

pom-pom tips

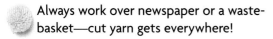 Always work over newspaper or a waste-basket—cut yarn gets everywhere!

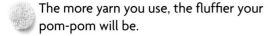 The more yarn you use, the fluffier your pom-pom will be.

Trim only the outside edges of a pom-pom. If you trim too deeply, it may fall apart.

Small sewing scissors work best for these projects.

To shape pom-pom animals, look at the different angles of each animal in the photos. Lightly trim yarn, check against our example, then trim again, if needed. Always trim where the pom-poms will touch so they'll glue together better.

To attach a chenille stem to a pom-pom, dip the end of the stem into glue and press it deep into the yarn. Hold until the stem sticks. Let dry.

To make most ears, you'll need to cut felt into a mousehole shape. Dip the straight edge of the felt into glue, press it against the pom-pom, and pinch it inward until it holds.

mixing colors
To mix colors, try these yarn tricks!

cow's body
On both A and B pairs, randomly mix white and black yarn.

rooster's body
On both A and B pairs, wrap black yarn just in the middle. Finish each one with white.

raccoon's head
On one A and B pair, wrap black yarn first, then finish with brown. On the other pair, wrap just brown yarn.

owl's body
On both A and B pairs, randomly mix tan and brown yarns.

owl's head
On both A and B pairs, wrap a layer of tan yarn first, then cover with a layer of brown.

skunk's body
Make a white side with one A and B pair and a black side with the other A and B pair.

mouse

You will need:

tan yarn

blue & purple makers

scissors

pink & brown felt

glue

1 pink premade mini
 pom-pom

2 large seed beads

1. Make 1 tan pom-pom with blue maker and 1 with purple maker. Trim.

2. From felt, cut out ears and a tail as shown.

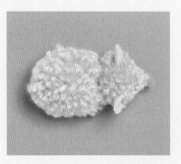

3. Glue pom-poms together. Glue on ears and a mini pom-pom for a nose.

4. Glue on bead eyes and the tail. Let mouse dry.

bunny

You will need:
white yarn
blue, purple & lime makers
scissors
white & pink felt
glue
2 large seed beads
1 pink premade mini
   pom-pom

1. Make 1 white pom-pom with blue maker, 1 with purple maker, and 1 with lime maker. Trim.

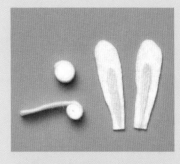

2. Cut out felt ears and pink "shading." Glue together. For front legs, roll 2 small felt strips, then glue closed.

3. Glue pom-poms together. Glue on the legs.

4. Glue on bead eyes and mini pom-pom for a nose.

5. Glue the ears to the head. Let bunny dry.

piglet

You will need:

pink yarn

blue & purple makers

scissors

dark pink felt

glue

2 dark pink plain
  chenille stems

2 large seed beads

1. Make 1 pink pom-pom with blue maker and 1 with purple maker. Trim.

2. Cut out felt ears. For a snout, roll a felt strip, then glue closed. Cut a chenille stem into 4 legs as shown.

3. Glue pom-poms together as shown. Cut and curl a chenille stem into a tail and glue it on.

4. Glue on bead eyes, ears, snout, and legs. Let pig dry.

sheep

You will need:

white yarn
blue & purple makers
scissors
1 black premade medium
 pom-pom
black & white felt
1 black plain chenille stem
glue
2 large seed beads
pink yarn scrap

1. Make 1 white pom-pom with blue maker and 1 with purple maker. Trim all pom-poms.

2. From felt, cut out ears, tail, and a tail spot. Glue spot to tail. Cut chenille stem into 4 legs as shown.

3. Glue pom-poms together as shown. Glue on premade medium pom-pom for a muzzle. Glue on bead eyes and tail.

4. Glue on ears and legs. Tie pink yarn into a bow around the neck. Let sheep dry.

polar bear

You will need:

white yarn
blue & lime makers
scissors
white & black felt
1 white fuzzy chenille stem
glue
1 black premade mini
   pom-pom
2 small seed beads

1. Make 1 white pom-pom with blue maker and 1 with lime maker. Trim.

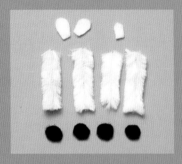

2. From felt, cut out ears, circles for paws, and a tail. Cut the chenille stem into 4 legs as shown.

3. Glue pom-poms together. Glue on the mini pom-pom nose, bead eyes, ears, legs, and tail.

4. Glue a paw onto each leg. Let polar bear dry.

duck

You will need:
yellow yarn
lime maker
scissors
1 yellow premade large
  pom-pom
orange & yellow felt
glue
2 large seed beads

1. Make 1 yellow pom-pom with lime maker. Trim all pom-poms.

2. From felt, cut out 2 beaks and 2 wings as shown.

3. Glue pom-poms together as shown. Glue on beaks.

4. Glue on bead eyes and wings. Let duck dry.

squirrel

You will need:

brown yarn

purple & lime makers

scissors

1 tan premade medium
  pom-pom

brown felt

1 brown curly chenille stem
  (not included)

1 tan premade mini
  pom-pom

glue

3 large seed beads

1. Make 1 brown pom-pom with purple maker and 1 with lime maker. Trim all pom-poms.

2. From felt, cut out ears and a small brown circle. Cut a small piece of chenille stem into 2 front legs.

3. Glue pom-poms together as shown. Glue on mini pom-pom nose, bead eyes, ears, and front legs.

4. Curl rest of chenille stem, and glue it up squirrel's back for a tail.

5. For an acorn, glue circle to premade medium pom-pom, then glue a bead on top. Glue acorn to chest. Let squirrel dry.

puppy

You will need:

tan yarn

blue & purple makers

scissors

1 brown premade medium
   pom-pom

brown felt

1 brown plain chenille stem

1 brown premade mini
   pom-pom

glue

2 large seed beads

1. Make 1 tan pom-pom with blue maker and 1 with purple maker. Trim all pom-poms.

2. Cut out felt ears and paws. Cut chenille stem into tail, 2 short legs, and 2 long legs. Fold back legs as shown.

3. Glue pom-poms together as shown. Glue on premade medium pom-pom for muzzle and mini pom-pom for nose.

4. Glue on bead eyes, ears, legs, and tail. Glue paws to back legs. Let puppy dry.

kitten

You will need:

white yarn
blue & purple makers
scissors
white & pink felt
1 white fuzzy chenille stem
white thread
glue
2 white premade small
pom-poms
1 pink premade mini
pom-pom
2 large seed beads

1. Make 1 white pom-pom with blue maker and 1 with purple maker. Trim.

2. Cut out felt ears and paws. Cut chenille stem into front legs and tail. Cut 2 pieces of thread.

3. Glue pom-poms together. Glue on small white pom-poms for a muzzle.

4. Glue thread above muzzle for whiskers. Glue mini pom-pom over whiskers.

5. Glue on bead eyes, ears, legs, and tail. Glue paws to legs. Let kitten dry.

elephant

You will need:
gray yarn
purple & lime makers
scissors
gray & pink felt
2 gray plain chenille stems
glue
chenille stem piece
2 large seed beads

1. Make 1 gray pom-pom with purple maker and 1 with lime maker. Trim.

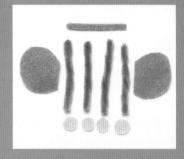

2. Cut out felt ears, foot pads, and tail. Twist both chenille stems together, then cut into 4 legs.

3. Glue pom-poms together. Glue on ears, bead eyes, tail, legs, and foot pads.

4. For a trunk, wrap a felt square around a chenille stem piece. Trim stem, then glue closed.

5. Bend and shape trunk, then glue to head. Let elephant dry.

camel

You will need:

tan yarn

blue & lime makers

scissors

1 tan premade small
  pom-pom

1 tan premade medium
  pom-pom

tan & brown felt

2 tan plain chenille stems

glue

2 small seed beads

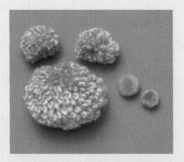

1. Make 2 tan pom-poms with blue maker and 1 with lime maker. Trim all pom-poms.

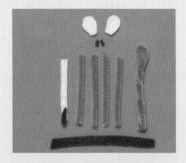

2. Cut felt ears, nostrils, tail, spot, and hoof strip. Glue spot to tail. Cut 1 stem into legs. Cut other stem to 8 inches, then bend and twist.

3. For head, glue premade small and medium pom-poms together as shown. Glue twisted stem to head for neck.

4. Glue pom-poms together as shown. Glue neck to body. Add nostrils to head.

5. Wrap hoof strip around a leg and trim. Repeat on remaining legs. Glue on legs, ears, tail, and bead eyes. Let camel dry.

monkey

You will need:

tan yarn

purple maker

scissors

1 tan premade medium
  pom-pom

1 tan premade large
  pom-pom

1 brown curly chenille stem
  (not included)

brown, pink & tan felt

glue

2 small seed beads

1. Make 1 tan pom-pom with purple maker. Trim all pom-poms.

2. Cut chenille stem into arms and legs. From felt, cut out ears, eyelids, mouth, paws, and tail.

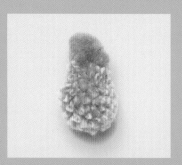

3. Glue premade large pom-pom to handmade pom-pom. Glue on pre-made medium pom-pom for monkey's muzzle.

4. Glue on mouth, eyelids, tail, bead eyes, ears, arms, legs, and paws. Let monkey dry.

poodle

You will need:

white yarn

blue & purple makers

scissors

white & pink felt

glue

1 white bumpy chenille stem

2 white premade medium
  pom-poms

2 small seed beads

1 black premade mini
  pom-pom

pink yarn scrap

1. Make 1 white pom-pom with blue maker and 1 with purple maker. Trim.

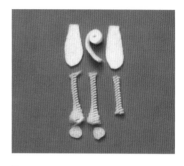

2. Cut out felt ears and paws. For a snout, roll felt strip, then glue closed. Cut chenille stem into front legs and tail.

3. Glue pom-poms together, adding 1 premade medium pom-pom in between.

4. Glue 1 premade medium pom-pom to tail. Glue on bead eyes, ears, legs, tail, and paws.

5. Glue on snout and mini pom-pom for a nose. Make and glue on yarn bows. Let poodle dry.

chickens

You will need:

yellow, white & black yarn

blue, purple & lime makers

scissors

orange, yellow, white & red felt

glue

1 yellow premade medium pom-pom

2 white premade large pom-poms

2 small seed beads

4 large seed beads

1. Make 1 yellow pom-pom with blue maker, 1 white with purple maker, and 1 mixed (see page 9) with lime maker. Trim.

2. From felt, make 6 bird feet, 3 beaks, 2 sets of tail feathers, 2 wings, and 1 comb as shown.

3. Glue premade pom-poms to handmade pom-poms as shown.

4. Glue on bead eyes, beaks, feet, tail feathers, wings, and comb. Let chick, hen, and rooster dry.

skunk

You will need:

white & black yarn

lime maker

scissors

1 black premade x-large pom-pom (not included)

white & black felt

glue

1 black fuzzy chenille stem

2 small seed beads

1 white fuzzy chenille stem

1 white premade mini pom-pom

1. Make 1 mixed pom-pom (see page 9) with lime maker. Trim all pom-poms.

2. Cut out felt eyes and front legs. For back legs, roll felt strips, then glue closed. Loop black stem to form tail.

3. Glue pom-poms together. Glue on teardrop shapes and beads for eyes.

4. Glue on tail. Glue a white chenille stem along back of skunk to end of tail.

5. Glue on legs and mini pom-pom for a nose. Let skunk dry.

COW

You will need:

white & black yarn
blue & lime makers
scissors
1 black premade medium
   pom-pom
black, white & pink felt
1 white fuzzy chenille stem
glue
2 large seed beads

1. Make 1 white pom-pom with blue maker and 1 mixed (see page 9) with lime maker. Trim all pom-poms.

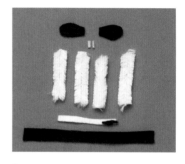

2. Cut out felt ears, nostrils, hoof strip, tail, and tail spot. Glue spot to tail. Cut chenille stem into 4 legs.

3. Glue pom-poms together. Glue on premade pom-pom for a muzzle. Add nostrils and ears.

4. Wrap hoof strip around bottom of leg, then trim. Repeat with remaining legs. Glue on legs, tail, and bead eyes. Let cow dry.

raccoon

You will need:

brown & black yarn

blue & lime makers

scissors

brown & tan felt

1 black plain chenille stem

glue

2 small seed beads

2 tan premade mini
  pom-poms

1 black premade medium
  pom-pom

1 brown premade medium
  pom-pom

1 black premade small
  pom-pom

1 brown premade small
  pom-pom

1. Make 1 mixed pom-pom (see page 9) with blue maker and 1 brown with lime maker. Trim.

2. Cut out felt ears, "mask," and 2 paws. Cut chenille stem into front legs.

3. Glue pom-poms together. Glue on mask, bead eyes, a mini pom-pom for nose, legs, ears, and paws.

4. For a tail, glue 5 premade pom-poms together in a row. Let raccoon dry.

owl

You will need:
brown, tan & cream yarn
purple & lime makers
scissors
black & brown felt
glue

1. Make 2 mixed pom-poms (see page 9) with purple and lime makers. Trim.

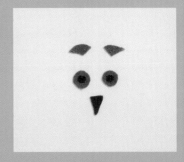

2. From felt, cut out eyes, eyeballs, tuft feathers, and beak. Glue eyeballs to eyes.

3. Glue pom-poms together as shown. Press yarn apart to make eye sockets.

4. Glue on eyes, beak, and tufts. Let owl dry.

go wild!

Hunt around the house for fun animal accents. Try peacock feathers, special fuzzy yarns for fur, wire for feet, eggshells for nests—your zoo is up to you!

Sound your trum**pet**! Walk the red car**pet**!
Send your cutest pom-pom **pet** photos to:

Pom-Pom Pet Editor
American Girl
8400 Fairway Place
Middleton, WI 53562

(Sorry, photos can't be returned.
All comments and suggestions
received by American Girl may be
used without compensation or
acknowledgment.)

Here are some other American Girl books you might like:

❑ I read it.

❑ I read it.

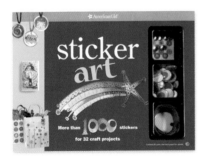

❑ I read it.

❑ I read it.